To those who died for the idea – then and now

DANIEL SCHWARTZ, 1955-

THE GREAT WALL OF CHINA

with 159 duotone photographs and 10 maps

Including 'The Wall and the Books' by Jorge Luis Borges
The Great Wall in History by Luo Zhewen

THAMES AND HUDSON

PAGE ONE Hebei, Jinshanling Section. Gansu, Jiuquan Section.
Two sections of the Great Wall of the Ming Dynasty, separated by 1500
miles of Wall

'The Wall and the Books', by Jorge Luis Borges.
Jorge Luis Borges: *Labyrinths*. Copyright © 1962, 1964 by New
Directions Publishing Corporation. Translated by James E. Irby.
Reprinted by permission of New Directions Publishing Corporation.
U.S. and Canadian rights.

© 1990 Thames and Hudson Ltd, London
Photographs © 1990 Daniel Schwartz

First published in the United States in 1990 by
Thames and Hudson Inc., 500 Fifth Avenue,
New York, New York 10110

Library of Congress Catalog Card Number 89-50637

Printed and bound in Japan

CONTENTS

THE WALL AND THE BOOKS

He, whose long wall the wand'ring Tartar bounds . . . DUNCIAD, II, 76

I read, some days past, that the man who ordered the erection of the almost infinite wall of China was that first Emperor, Shih Huang Ti, who also decreed that all books prior to him be burned. That these two vast operations – the five to six hundred leagues of stone opposing the barbarians, the rigorous abolition of history, that is, of the past – should originate in one person and be in some way his attributes inexplicably satisfied and, at the same time, disturbed me. To investigate the reasons for that emotion is the purpose of this note.

Historically speaking, there is no mystery in the two measures. A contemporary of the wars of Hannibal, Shih Huang Ti, king of Tsin, brought the Six Kingdoms under his rule and abolished the feudal system; he erected the wall, because walls were defences; he burned the books, because his opposition invoked them to praise the emperors of olden times. Burning books and erecting fortifications is a common task of princes; the only thing singular in Shih Huang Ti was the scale on which he operated. Such is suggested by certain Sinologists, but I feel that the facts I have related are something more than an exaggeration or hyperbole of trivial dispositions. Walling in an orchard or a garden is ordinary, but not walling in an empire. Nor is it banal to pretend that the most traditional of races renounce the memory of its past, mythical or real. The Chinese had three thousand years of chronology (and during those years the Yellow Emperor and Chuang Tsu and Confucius and Lao Tzu) when Shih Huang Ti ordered that history begin with him.

Shih Huang Ti had banished his mother for being a libertine; in his stern justice the orthodox saw nothing but an impiety; Shih Huang Ti, perhaps, wanted to obliterate the canonical books because they accused him; Shih Huang Ti, perhaps, tried to abolish the entire past in order to abolish one single memory: his mother's infamy. (Not in an unlike manner did a king of Judea have all male children killed in order to kill one.) This conjecture is worthy of attention, but tells us nothing about the wall, the second part of the myth. Shih Huang Ti, according to the historians, forbade that death be mentioned and sought the elixir of immortality and secluded himself in a figurative palace .

containing as many rooms as there are days in the year; these facts suggest that the wall in space and the fire in time were magic barriers designed to halt death. All things long to persist in their being, Baruch Spinoza has written; perhaps the Emperor and his sorcerers believed that immortality is intrinsic and that decay cannot enter a closed orb. Perhaps the Emperor tried to recreate the beginning of time and called himself The First, so as to be really first, and called himself Huang Ti, so as to be in some way Huang Ti, the legendary emperor who invented writing and the compass. The latter, according to the *Book of Rites*, gave things their true name; in a parallel fashion, Shih Huang Ti boasted, in inscriptions which endure, that all things in his reign would have the name which was proper to them. He dreamt of founding an immortal dynasty; he ordered that his heirs be called Second Emperor, Third Emperor, Fourth Emperor, and so on to infinity. . . . I have spoken of a magical purpose; it would also be fitting to suppose that erecting the wall and burning the books were not simultaneous acts. This (depending on the order we select) would give us the image of a king who began by destroying and then resigned himself to preserving, or that of a disillusioned king who destroyed what he had previously defended. Both conjectures are dramatic, but they lack, as far as I know, any basis in history. Herbert Allen Giles tells that those who hid books were branded with a red-hot iron and sentenced to labour until the day of their death on the construction of the outrageous wall. This information favours or tolerates another interpretation. Perhaps the wall was a metaphor, perhaps Shih Huang Ti sentenced those who worshipped the past to a task as immense, as gross and as useless as the past itself. Perhaps the wall was a challenge and Shih Huang Ti thought: 'Men love the past and neither I nor my executioners can do anything against that love, but someday there will be a man who feels as I do and he will efface my memory and be my mirror and not know it.' Perhaps Shih Huang Ti walled in his empire because he knew that it was perishable and destroyed the books because he understood that they were sacred books, in other words, books that teach what the entire universe or the mind of every man teaches. Perhaps the burning of the libraries and the erection of the wall are operations, which in some secret way cancel each other.

The tenacious wall which at the moment, and at all moments, casts its system of shadows over lands I shall never see, is the shadow of a Caesar who ordered the most reverent of nations to burn its past; it is plausible that this idea moves us in itself, aside from the conjectures it allows. (Its virtue may lie in the opposition of constructing and destroying on an enormous scale.) Generalizing from the preceding case, we could infer that *all* forms have their virtue in themselves and not in any conjectural 'content'. This would concord with the thesis of Benedetto Croce; already Pater in 1877 had affirmed that all arts aspire to the state of music, which is pure form. Music, states of happiness, mythology, faces belaboured by time, certain twilights and certain places try to tell us something, or have said something we should have missed, or are about to say something; this imminence of a revelation which does not occur is, perhaps, the aesthetic phenomenon.

JORGE LUIS BORGES
(*translated by James E. Irby*)

Guyuan, Ningxia.
The first Great Wall, built between 217 and 210 BC under the Qin Dynasty.

INTRODUCTION

The Great Wall of China cannot be photographed. It is not a line of stones on the ground. It is an idea. It is not even a wall. It is many walls, built over roughly 2000 years by different dynasties. We tend to think that 'China' surrounded itself by a wall. It was rather that the different peoples who in the course of history came to constitute China put up walls of their own. Invaders from the north would overrun one stretch of wall and erect another further out. Eventually these sections were joined together to make the wall we know.

So the search for the Great Wall is essentially the search for an idea. Great Walls were built, destroyed, buried under sand-dunes. Parts are still there to be discovered. To make a picture of this idea I had to travel 25,000 kilometres, roughly five times the length of the main wall. It took me eight months. Of course the task was impossible.

I wanted to do it because it was impossible. I wanted to find out where the boundaries of the impossible lay, and how close I could get to them. The project of documenting the wall was a pretext. What mattered was the experience. When I started on the journey I knew there was no destination and no end. But the route was determined; there was no way of deviating from the Wall. At the same time, it was not just a matter of following it. The Wall was often an obstacle to the journey, something to be overcome.

Anyone who wants to create has to test himself against something new. The Great Wall was such a test for me. As an experience it is over. The book is the result, the experience brought out into the open and made into something different, something independent of the experience, something with its own reality. The experience remains private to me, and I am only just beginning to understand it.

What experience was I hoping for? I don't think I had any specific expectation. It was like going into a tunnel. You know that it is going to be dark, but you don't know how dark, or what you might stumble over or when you will see light at the other end. I wanted to find out what I was capable of in those circumstances. It is one thing to function and be creative in one's normal surroundings, quite another when one is totally cut off from everything that is familiar. So I wanted an answer, and the photographs I took are that answer.

Qijiapu, Benxi, Liaoning.
Apparition.

I was on my own. I had drivers and interpreters, but no companion, with the exception of a small stretch where I was accompanied by Dieter Bachmann of *Du* magazine. I could not have done it without the help of Professor Luo Zhewen of the Ministry of Culture in Beijing. He supported me in every way he could. Wherever I had letters of introduction from him I felt quite secure. In between I was left to cope as best I could. You cannot travel wherever you like in China. There are travel permits, and as I later discovered I ought to have had them, but no one was willing or able to organize my journey because no one knew exactly what could be done. Some things are neither allowed nor forbidden – you just can't do them. And of course there are some areas that are closed to foreigners.

So you never know what is going to happen. You are completely at the mercy of local officials. Or just luck. One day you are arrested or confined to your hotel room. The next you are the guest of honour at a banquet. If you are arrested in China you are given a lecture on your conduct. It is the modern equivalent of the old Chinese 'kow-tow' to authority. The bureaucracy in China is another kind of wall that confronts the outsider.

More than once I could only glimpse what I wanted to photograph in the distance through the windscreen. But the next time round, maybe on the other side, I was allowed to take it.

I should have felt more isolated without the driver and interpreter who came with me. We became a sort of community, thrown together by fate. They tried to understand my strange ways of doing things and after a while they managed to adapt my instructions to the prevailing conditions very intelligently. They thought of ways of getting to places that I could not have managed on my own, and in my turn I would give up trying to see others in order not to make things too difficult for them.

I knew exactly where I wanted to go. I had precise longitudes and latitudes. The question was how to get there. I was continually in search of information. Directions given by a solitary cyclist on the steppes might save us a hundred kilometres, or the opposite. We would find streets swept away or police barriers forcing us to make long detours. Sometimes I would reach the spot of which I had an illustration only to find that the wall and towers had been submerged under an artificial lake. My illustration was out of date. No one had bothered to tell me because no one expected I would ever get that far.

Reliable maps, especially of the provinces and outlying parts of China, are harder to find than the roads once you get there. I had collected whatever I could, from American flight maps and Chinese atlases, and the driver had a few more detailed maps that were not generally available. Sometimes, officially, there was no map, but then we would find it displayed in some place along the road, and I had to make a hurried sketch from it. The driver measured the distance by rolling a coin on the map.

I saw a China quite different from that seen by other foreigners. I met no tourists. My China was not beautiful, it was ugly. Not a country asking to be photographed. Not easy and not friendly. I felt that I had to fight to produce my pictures, against the atmosphere of China, against the whole character of Chinese thought, against Chinese topography, against Chinese light. Often it was the last light of the day – not because I had chosen it for the exciting shadows it produced, but because it was only after I had talked and waited and talked again and been given drinks and talked yet again and finally made my point – only then could I go and climb to where I wanted to be and take my photographs.

This real China did actually make a very deep impression on me, but I did not put it into this book except insofar as the Wall reflected it. The Wall was my theme. As a photographer, I deliberately shut myself off from every other. If I photographed people they somehow had to do with the Wall. I took many photographs of women. The way they looked seemed to me to be like those mothers, wives or daughters who had seen their sons, husbands or fathers dragged away from them to work on the construction of the Great Wall, who hoped for their return but knew that only a few would ever come home.

Today, though deprived of its age-old function, the Wall still binds human fates together, each man assigned to a quite specific segment, whether it be through his work as historian, archaeologist or any of the other workers engaged in researching and maintaining the ancient monuments or whether it be as a shepherd or farmer burrowing into the rampart to provide a retreat for himself and his household animals on the icebound loessial plateau or piling up his stock of maize and fuel against the wall of warm and reddish-grey bricks. I think also of personal friendships and private encounters – and of the dead man.

It was at a point on the mountain ridge from where you can see the Temple of Meng Jiangnu with the Looking-for-the-Husband Rock. According to legend, Meng Jiangnu's husband had been forced to build the first Great Wall under Qin Huangdi. The different flowers blossomed and died and with them the numerous seasons of the Chinese calendar, each slightly different from the one before, passed in slow succession. Winter came and still Meng Jiangnu had had no news. And so she set off to take her husband warm clothes. She walked a thousand *li*, stopping again and again to ask the way, until at last she came to the place where her husband had been employed and where he had died of exhaustion. As she wept, the wall broke open, revealing her husband's body. The dead man whom I saw lay on a shelf of rock; there was no terror in seeing him. There he lay, as firmly anchored in time and space as the chessboard that soldiers had carved in the stone beside the watchtower, as clear as the ridge of the wall that grew out of the landscape and as plain as the path which led to the next pass. What this image came to encapsulate was something that the annals of history justify us in thinking – that hundreds and thousands will lay down their lives for the sake of an idea.

It is very difficult for a Westerner, to whom a wall is just a wall, to empathize with the beliefs that the Chinese attach to it. He has first to understand *Chi. Chi* – in reality the earth's magnetism – is a mystical force that flows through every object of nature and affects people in this life and the next. Nothing that man adds to nature must interfere with the rhythms of *Chi*. Everything must breathe its harmony. Certain magical places and streams are sanctified by it. When somebody dies, the time and place of the burial are governed by *Chi*. We saw such a burial close to the Wall, and became involved with it in unexpected ways.

Those who built the Wall were deeply conscious of *Chi. Chi*-veins are also known as dragon-lines. Mountains symbolize peaceful dragons and the Great Wall has always been an embodiment of that idea. When the Wall was built the natural dragon got an artificial spine. Legend has it that General Meng Tian, the builder of the first Great Wall, was overthrown by a conspiracy and made to drink poison; he accepted his fate as punishment for the fact that in building it he had inadvertently broached one of the dragon-lines beneath the earth.

The more one studies, ponders and photographs the Great Wall the more multi-layered its symbolism grows. Even as a military defence it is as much psychological as functional. The Chinese think in terms of walls. They build walls round their houses. They surround their dining tables with screens. They are at present in the midst of planting the Green Great Wall, a wall of trees as a protection against the wind from the north and erosion of the steppe. It is interesting to see what happens in those places where there was no military necessity for any wall at all, where the line runs along dizzy cliffs which no enemy could possibly scale. Yet here too a token wall had to exist, like the steps of a stony staircase sometimes hardly ten centimetres deep. The enemy sees it and says: 'I want

Huajialing, Dingxi County, Gansu.
Along the vanished Great Wall of the Qin Dynasty.

nothing to do with anyone who is capable of something like that.' In the same way, a Mongolian horseman, used to the open plains where he could ride at will, must have received a shock when he saw the black barrier blocking his path.

When I started I had a clear programme in my mind. I intended to compile an informative document combining fact and personal experience, starting at the Korean border and following the Wall along its entire course until I reached the point where it petered out into the desert, merging with the material from which it is made. I had fixed in my mind certain key points that would be essential, such as particular forks, important passes and gates. The reality has been different, less physically defined. Often the 'Wall' ran on when there was no recognizable wall to see. In the middle of the desert there may be nothing but heaps of mud-brick every few kilometres, the remains of beacon towers. From the top of these crumbling piles there is nothing to see and only one's own shadow to photograph. This photograph becomes part of my 'reconstruction' of the Wall, as well as the photograph of the tracks of our car as we follow it through the snow.

Intimate contact with the subject of my work was important to me. So there are no photographs here taken from the air. That would have distanced me from the Wall, raised me above it. On the other hand, I was very often under it, and under its spell. My photographs reflect this feeling, this knowledge; they are the expression of a desired confrontation, here and now. The aesthetic of my photographs is thus very different from that of the Chinese, for whom the Wall is a symbolic image. In photographs, in watercolours and murals and in the background of studio portraits, they love to show it floating in a sea of blossoms or billowing clouds in such a way that its relation to the spectator is left utterly vague.

Only in my last picture is the Wall virtually a Fata Morgana, but you still sense that feet have trodden here. Where does the track go? It could go on; the country ahead is flat; but it does not. Whoever made it turned on his heel. Perhaps he kicked a pebble away and said to himself: 'This is the end . . . an end . . .' And then, 'Indeed there is no end'.

One experience ends. Another could begin, one which would certainly be made all on one's own. . . . Beyond that point one would not think of photography.

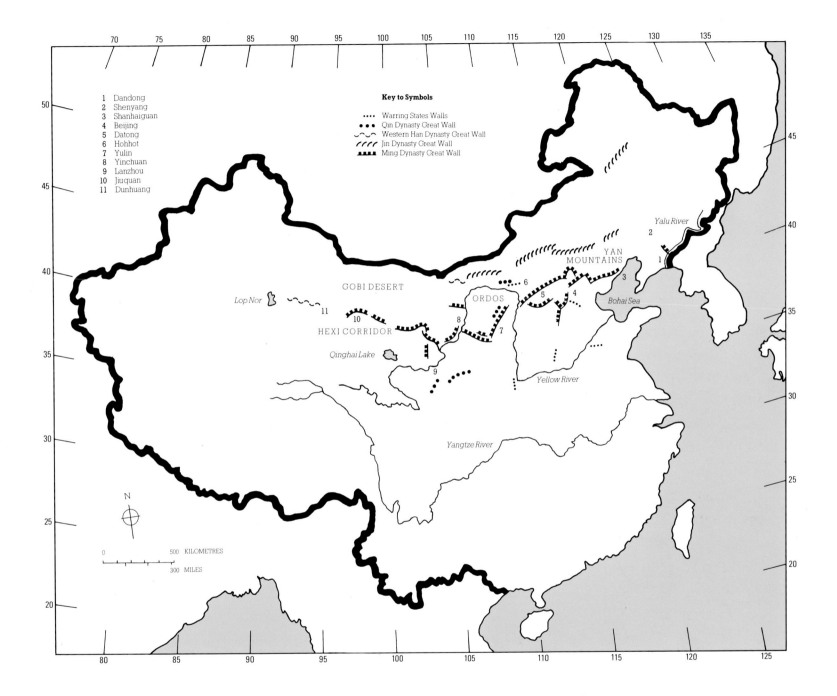

Key to Symbols

⋯⋯ Warring States Walls
●●● Qin Dynasty Great Wall
〜〜〜 Western Han Dynasty Great Wall
ﬀﬀﬀ Jin Dynasty Great Wall
▬▬▬ Ming Dynasty Great Wall

Yalu River

YAN
MOUNTAINS

GOBI DESERT

Lop Nor

ORDOS

Bohai Sea

HEXI CORRIDOR

Qinghai Lake

Yellow River

Yangtze River

N

0   500 KILOMETRES

300 MILES

The remaining parts of the Great Walls.

PART I

SECTIONS I–IV

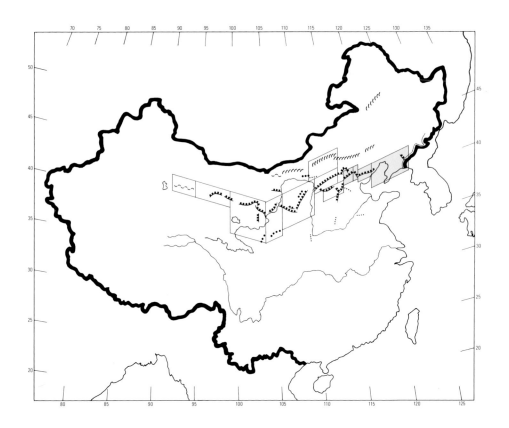

Near sea level. Yalu River, Chinese-Korean border, Kuandian County,
Liaoning.
Mount Hu, the eastern end of the Ming Great Wall.

SECTION I

The Other End
From the Yalu River to 'The First Pass Under Heaven'

Stages of Construction

1st: around 1400
2nd: around 1614

Zhangdian, Kuandian County, Liaoning.
First tracks of the Wall.

40°26′N 124°49′E

Mount Yiwulu, Beizhen County, Liaoning.
Beacon tower.

Fuli, Suizhong County, Liaoning.
Jiumenkou Section.

40°14'N 119°48'E

Qinhuangdao, Hebei.
Sandaoguan Section, the first pass.

40°07′N 119°45′E

Sandaoguan Section, near the second pass.
A path beneath the wall leads down to Jiaoshanguan. On the rock beside the
tower soldiers had carved a chess-board.

40°07′N 119°45′E

Sandaoguan, where the dead man lies.

40°07'N 119°45'E

Shanhaiguan, Hebei.
'The First Pass Under Heaven'.

40°00′N 119°45′E

Shenyang, Liaoning

Beizhen, Liaoning

Benxi, Liaoning.

Dandong, Liaoning.

40°07′N 124°23′E

Laolongtou, Shanhaiguan, Hebei.
Where the Great Wall met the sea.

SECTION II

The Continuity and the Great Wall
From the Bohai Sea to the Yan Mountains

Stages of Construction

1st: 1368–1378
2nd: 1568–1582

Qianshuihe, Xinglong County, Hebei.
Lijiazhai, Kuancheng County, Hebei.
Dongxinzhuang, Qian'an County, Hebei.
Three of seventy-three passes.

Yiyuankou, Qinhuangdao, Hebei.
Anyingzhai, Xinglong County, Hebei.
Simatai, Miyun County, Beijing.
Life along the Wall.

Seventy-three passes, thirteen visits.

Passes seen and unseen. Incidents of history and of the journey:
*Laolongtou (destroyed by the Eight Power Allied Army in 1909; restored in
1987) – Jiaoshanguan (brickmakers) – Sandaoguan (dead man) – Jiumenkou
(peasants)* – Chengzegukou – *Dongjiakou (threshers) – Yiyuankou (William
Edgar Geil, 1908, farrier)* – Nazegukou – Weizegukou – Guchegukou –
Jiangunlingkou – Pingliankou – Jingshankou – Hudonggukou – Taolingkou –
Linjiakou – Xilinkou – Helinkou – *Donxinzhang (interpreter) – Lengkou
(damaged by earthquake, 1975)* – Shimengukou – Baiyanggukou –
Zayazekou – Chengzelingkou – Yumulingkou – Jingshankou – Dongjiakou –
Tiemenguan – *Xifengkou (submerged, 1976)* – Chengguankou – *Panjiakou
(submerged, 1976) – Lijiazhai (porter)* – Dongchangukou – Hongshankou –
Xi'ngangukou – Madigukou – Zaijiagukou – Lewengukou – Jianjiagukou –
Sanzhaigukou – Shapogukou – Lengshuitoukou – Tang'ankou – Nianyukou –
Malangguan – Gujiangyukou – Jingshanlingkou – Chedaoyukou –
Huangyaguan (reconstructed, 1986/7) – Jiangjunguan (mourners) –
Heishuiwan'kou – Huangsunyukou – Dayuzhaikou – Nanshuiyukou –
Beishuiyukou – *Anyingzhai (billiard players)* – Huangmenkou – *Qianshuihe
(alone)* – Xiaohuangyakou – Dahuangyakou – Dazhongyukou –
Zuomagankou – Nanyugoukou – Shanxiangyukou – Heiyuguankou –
Hanerlingkou – Taobanlingkou – Dujiangkou – *Simatai (shepherd)* –
Bolinggankou – Longwangyukou – *Jinshanling (soldier)* – Gubeikou
(damaged by Red Guards, 1970-74).

The Gubeikou Twin
Towers.
This photograph was
bought in the 1930s by
my grandfather. The
Chinese authorities will
make use of it in their
planned restoration of
the buildings.

The dormitory at
Gubeikou.

40°42′N 117°09′E

Simatai, Miyun County, Beijing.
Wall on wall.

SECTION III

Simatai – Jinshanling – Gubeikou

Stages of Construction

1st: 1368–1378
2nd: 1568–1582

Simatai, Tower 12.
Looking towards Jinshanling.

40°40'N 117°17'E

Simatai, Tower 14.

Simatai.
Parapet with arrow-slits.

40°40′N 117°17′E

Simatai.
The inscription on the brick reads 'Made by the Shitang Route Army, 5th
year of Wanli': that is, this section of the Wall was built by an army unit from
Shandong in 1577 during the reign of the Emperor Shenzhong.

40°40'N 117°17'E

About 3200 feet above sea level.
Simatai, Tower 16, on the summit.

40°40′N 117°17′E

Simatai.
Restoration work is carried out by people from the neighbouring villages.

40°40′N 117°17′E

40°40'N 117°17'E

Bakeshiying, Luanping County, Hebei.
View towards Simatai from Jinshanling.

40°43'N 117°15'E

Jinshanling.
Zhu Zhengxiu, one of the men who built a fire when it was cold . . . who called
over slopes and valleys to their wives in invisible villages to bring water . . .
who first saw a snake . . . who knew every step of their wall . . . who made
these photographs possible.

40°43′N 117°15′E

Jinshanling.
Looking towards Gubeikou.

40°43′N 117°15′E

Miyun County, Beijing.
Gubeikou Section.

Ling Gung Temple
in Gubeikou village.

Miyun County, Beijing.
Gubeikou Section.

Backyard and view of the
fortification wall round
the Gubeikou pass.

40°42′N 117°09′E

40°38′N 116°52′E

Beimaguan, Miyun County, Beijing.

SECTION IV

As the Dragon Winds

Stages of Construction

1st: 1368–1378
2nd: 1455
3rd: 1568–1582
4th: before 1619

Huairou County, Beijing.
Mutianyu Section.

40°25′N 116°35′E

Huairou County, Beijing.
Jiankou Section, looking eastwards.

Huairou County, Beijing.
Jiankou Section, looking westwards.

40°26′N 116°33′E

Huairou County, Beijing, Jiankou.
The cliffs of Jiankou.

40°26'N 116°33'E

About 2600 feet.
Badaling, Changping County, Beijing.
The Qinglongqiao Line.

The Badaling – Juyongguan – Nankou Valley.
The shortest route from the Mongolian plain to the Chinese heartland and
Beijing. It has been fortified since the Warring States Period. Among those
who have broken through in the course of the centuries was the army of
Ghenghis Khan in 1213.

40°20′N 116°00′E

PART II

SECTIONS V–VII

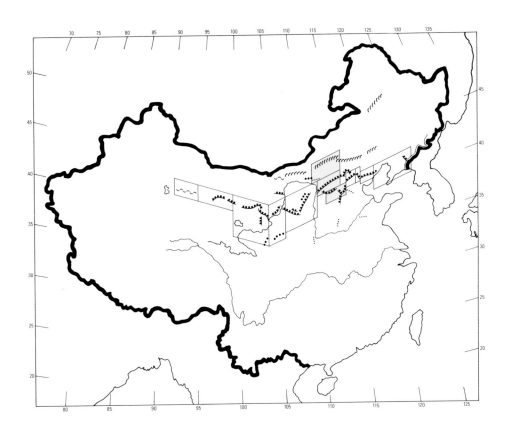

Juyongguan, Changping County, Beijing.
'Cloud Terrace', 1345, Yuan Dynasty. The archway is engraved with a text
from the Dharani Sutra in Sanskrit, Tibetan, 'p'ags-pa Mongolian, Uighur,
Western Xia and Chinese.

40°17′N 116°03′E

SECTION V

The Inner Great Wall

Stages of Construction

1st: 1368–1389
2nd: 1436–1452

Yanmenguan, Daixian County, Shanxi.
'Wild Geese Pass'.

Daixian, Shanxi.
'Gate of Peaceful Borders'.

39°11′N 112°50′E and 39°04′N 112°57′E

Laiyuan, Hebei.
A wall-builder's chisel marks.

Laiyuan, Hebei.
Branch of the Chajianling Section.

39°14′N 114°38′E

About 6000 feet above sea level.
Yanmenguan, Daixian County, Shanxi.
Record of repair work done on the Ming fort under the Qing Dynasty.

39°11′N 112°50′E

Xinguangwu, Shanyin County, Shanxi.
Beacon tower and part of the Mount Yanmen Section.

39°12'N 112°47'E

Mount Yanmen Section.
View from the summit. In the plain is the Guangwu Fort, built under the Jin
Dynasty (1115/1234), and the tombs of soldiers of the Song army killed in 980
fighting against the Khitans of the Liao Dynasty.

39°12'N 112°47'E

Datong, Shanxi.

SECTION VI

From Datong to the Yellow River

Stages of Construction

1st: 1403–1452
2nd: 1546

Yungang, Datong, Shanxi.

40°06′N 113°10′E

Datong, Shanxi.

Datong, Shanxi.

Datong, Shanxi.
Yungang Caves (453-459, Northern Wei Dynasty), Cave 18.

40°06′N 113°08′E

Xinrongzhen, Datong, Shanxi.
The second defence line.

Zhumabu, Datong, Shanxi.
The Outer Great Wall.
From Hongzhibu to Zhumabu: The Wall runs along a river . . . the Datong-
Hohhot road goes through it . . . it is the frontier between Shanxi and Inner
Mongolia . . . the Beijing-Ulan Bator railway crosses it . . . it provides shelter
for a coffin . . . wild horses roam over it.

40°18'N 112°53'E

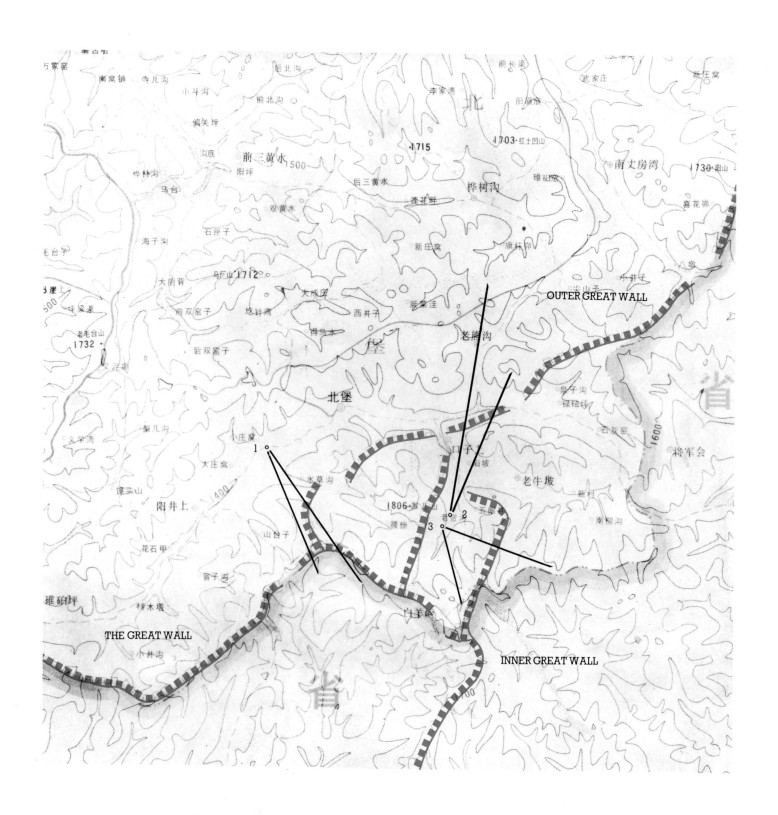

Beibu, Qingshuihe, Inner Mongolia.
The Western Bifurcation; 1, 2 and 3: the points where the photographs
opposite were taken.
1. Junction of the Inner and Outer Great Wall.
2. Towers of the Outer Great Wall.
3. Branch of the Inner Great Wall.

39°38′N 111°50′E

102

39°38′N 111°50′E

Shuiguanbao, Qingshuihe, Inner Mongolia.
Battle towers, looking east and (opposite) west

39°36'N 111°42'E

39°38'N 111°27'E

Laoninwang, Qingshuihe, Inner Mongolia.
About 3000 feet above sea level. Great Wall meets Yellow River.
Wall to tributary. Water to terraces. Tributary to river.

39°38′N 111°27′E

Binzhouhai, Hohhot, Inner Mongolia.
The Southern Wall of the Kingdom of Zhao (*c.* 300 BC, Warring States
Period). Farther ahead, in a field next to the Wall, preparations for a funeral.
Great grandfather's tomb is on the slope, grandfather's a little lower down.
The son's will be in the plain, next to the road.

SECTION VII

Inner Mongolia

Date of Construction

1190–1196

Bulitai, Siziwang Banner.
Along the Jin Great Wall.

42°11′N 111°47′E

Siziwang Banner.
Herdsmen's cellars.

Siziwang Banner.
Life along the Wall.

Somewhere, Siziwang Banner.

Sara Mörön Süme, Siziwang Banner.
Drinking songs.

42°03′N 111°32′E

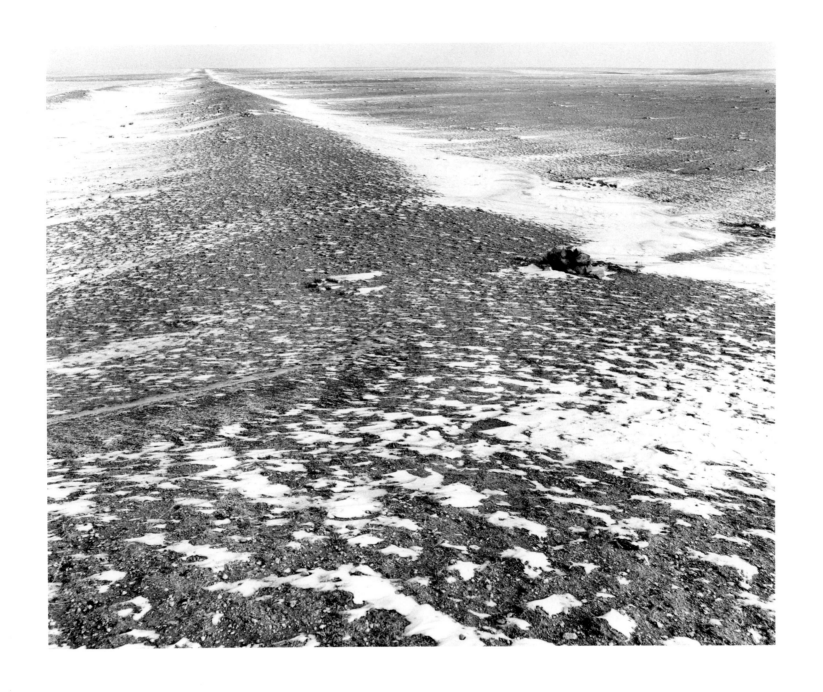

About 5500 feet above sea level.
Hongershumu Grassland, Siziwang Banner.
The Jin Great Wall. Built between 1190 and 1196, the Jin Great Wall runs
from the north of Inner Mongolia and Hebei as far as today's Mongolian
People's Republic and the USSR.

41°58′N 111°21′E

PART III

SECTIONS VIII–IX

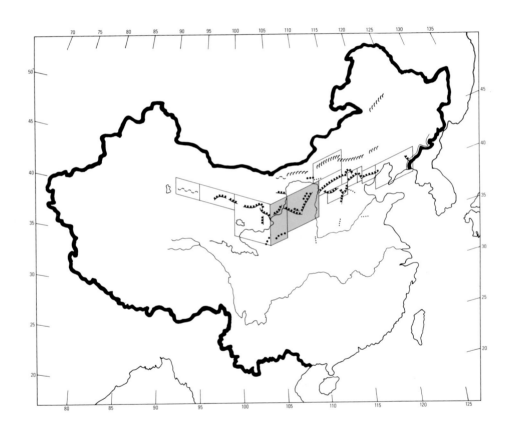

Maza, Jungar Banner, Inner Mongolia.
Great Wall meets Yellow River.

SECTION VIII

Across the Ordos

Stages of Construction

1st: 1436–1452
2nd: 1470–1480

Yijinhuolo, Dongsheng Banner, Inner Mongolia.
Aobao on the shrine of Ghenghis Khan.

Half-way point of the journey.

Yulin, a closed city. Arrested again. Urged to make a detour. Six hundred useless miles across the frozen loess plateau. Passing the tomb of General Mèng Tian (who supervised the construction of the first Great Wall) . . . passing drivers (who wrapped their sheepskin coats round the hood of the truck) . . . passing the headquarters of Mao Zedong (who modelled himself on the First Emperor) . . . passing the tomb of the Yellow Emperor (who flew to heaven) . . . passing drivers (who waited next to their collided trucks for the ice to melt) . . . passing the tomb of the First Emperor Qin Huangdi (who started the Great Wall).

Yulin, Shaanxi.
'The Terrace dominating the North'.

38°20′N 109°43′E

About 5000 feet above sea level.
Yanhuachang, Shaanxi.
Dingbian Section.

Yanchi, Ningxia.
Great Wall and city wall.

37°47'N 107°24'E

Goashawo, Yanchi County, Ningxia.
Maowusu Desert Section.

38°03'N 107°05'E

Niumaojing, Yanchi County, Ningxia.
Life along the Wall.

Shuidongao, Lingwu County, Ningxia.
The Northern Ordos Line.

38°18′N 106°29′E

Lingwu County, Ningxia.
Hengshanpu Fortress.

A funeral.

The young woman had committed suicide. We came into the village, just when the family started mourning in the street. Some days later, by chance, we come upon the funeral. Some of the relatives don't accept my being there; they say the soul of the dead will be disturbed. Others think my presence is a good sign. The geomancer has studied the horoscope and the topography and has decided upon a suitable site, which is open to beneficial streams of *ch'i* and protected from harmful ones. The husband is not convinced. They go on looking – small white dots in a landscape as bright as the sky above it. They want me to work out the best position for the burial. Sutras are being chanted at another tomb. We drive away; I see them open the yellow earth at the spot where the geomancer first placed his compass.

Wuda, Inner Mongolia.
Crossing the Yellow River.

SECTION IX

From the Helan Mountains to the First Great Wall

Stages of Construction

1st: 1436–1449
2nd: 1470–1480
3rd: 1524

Hongguozikou, Shizuishan, Ningxia.
Mount Helan Section.
Fissure caused by an earthquake.

38°51'N 106°10'E

Yuquanying, Ningxia.
Qingtonxia Section. The barrier of rammed earth, thirty feet high, runs
along the foot of the Helan Mountain Ridge.

38°08'N 105°46'E

38°25'N 106°03'E

Near Yinchuan, Ningxia.
Royal tombs of the Western Xia (1038-1227).

38°25′N 106°03′E

Zhongning County, Ningxia.
Clay figure, Shikong Grottoes (Tang Dynasty, 618-907).

Yellow River Gorge, Lingwu County, Ningxia.
The 'One Hundred and Eight' Pagoda (Yuan Dynasty, 1279-1368).

Yingshuiqiao, Zhongwei, Ningxia.
Tengger Desert Section.

37°31′N 105°07′E

About 4500 feet above sea level.
Liujiazhuang, Zhongning, Ningxia.
Zhongwei Section, descending to the plains of the Yellow River.

37°32′N 105°30′E

Muxiajia, Guyuan County, Ningxia.
The Great Wall of the Qin Dynasty – the first Great Wall. Between 217 and
210 BC more than a million labourers worked on it – convicts, soldiers,
peasants, children. Only three in ten ever returned. Today an irrigation
ditch runs along the Wall.

35°49′N 105°59′E

PART IV

SECTIONS X–XII

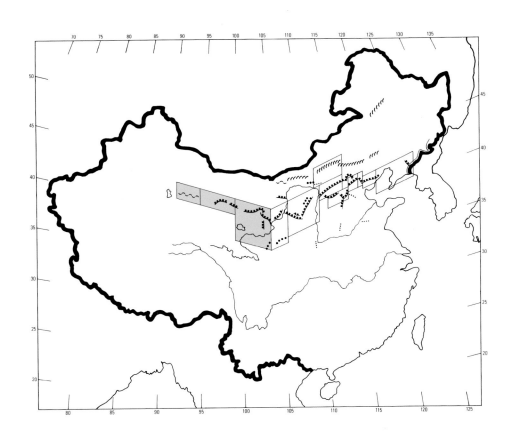

Tianzhu Tibetan Autonomous County, Gansu.
Section of the Lanzhou Loop.

SECTION X

In The Hexi Corridor

Stages of Construction

1st: after 1372
2nd: 1466–1480

Qinghai Lake, Qinghai.
Frozen waves.

36°34′N 100°38′E

Wuwei, Gansu.

Xiakou, Shandan County, Gansu.
Life along the Wall.

38°36′N 101°21′E

Hedazi, Gansu.
Yongchang Section.

Jingchuanzi, Gansu.
Yongchang Section.

38°20'N 101°53'E

Beihaizi, Yongchang County, Gansu.
Pagoda (Ming Dynasty, 15th century).

38°14′N 101°58′E

Xiakou, Gansu.
Shandan Section.

38°36′N 101°21′E

Xiakou, Gansu.
Shandan Section.
They are dots in the landscape where they herd their horses. They shelter
in caves hollowed out of the Wall. From its crenellations they keep watch.

38°38′N 101°17′E

About 7000 feet above sea level.
Shandan County, Gansu.
Crossing place of the Great Wall and the Gansu-Xinjiang Highway.

38°40′N 101°15′E

38°40′N 101°15′E

Yuanyang, Gansu.
Jiuquan Section.
Zhou Guangshi stops the Landrover. He turns back. The expression in his
eyes could mean: 'Do you really want to climb this tower too?' Or: 'If it's the
Gobi you want, you won't see any more from this one.' Or: 'They all look the
same.' Then he lights a 'Good Companion' and picks up a magazine
to read the short stories.

39°48′N 99°08′E

Yuanyang, Gansu.
Jiuquan Section.
Beacon tower.

SECTION XI

From the End of the Ming Great Wall to Dunhuang

Stages of Construction

1st: after 1372
2nd: 1466–1480
3rd: 1539–1540

Yemawanpu, Gansu.

Jiayuguan Section. From these structures smoke and fire signals were sent.

39°52'N 98°31'E

Jiayuguan, Gansu.
The Jiayuguan Barrier.
'Open Wall' and 'Hidden Wall'.

39°48′N 98°12′E

Jiayuguan, Gansu.
'The Strongest Fortress Under Heaven'.

39°40′N 97°58′E Looking east

The last watch tower: the end of the Ming Great Wall.

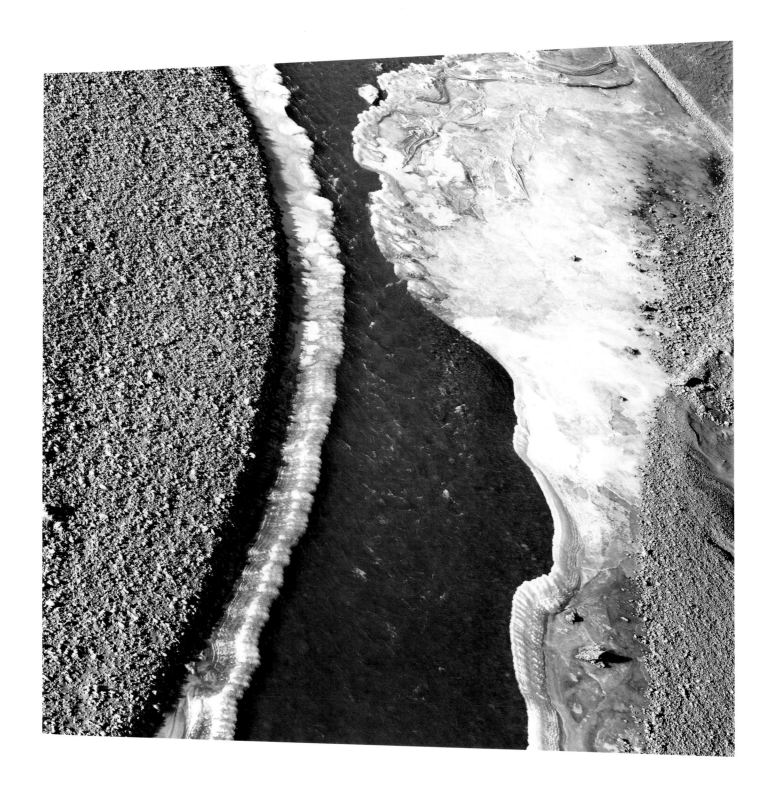

189

39°48′N 98°12′E

Yumen County . . . Anxi County . . . Dunhuang County . . . Gansu. Beacon
tower and gas station, beacon tower, fortress . . . coins, an earring, a skull . . .
fortress, beacon tower, air-field and tombs.

39°40'N 97°58'E Looking east

About 5800 feet above sea level.
Bulongji, Jiayuguan, Gansu.
Standing by the last watch tower. The Wall ends. The river passes by.
The first morning train is leaving.

39°40′N 97°58′E Looking west

Kunxin, Dunhuang County, Gansu.
Qing Dynasty beacon tower.

40°15′N 95°18′E

Mount Mingsha, Dunhuang County, Gansu.
Magao Grottoes (Northern Wei Dynasty, 386-534, to Yuan Dynasty,
1206-1368).

SECTION XII

Westward along the Han Great Wall

Date of Construction

c. 117–101 BC

Dunhuang, Gansu.
Mai Zhou Xiao (20) and Ma Yi Min (34).

40°08′N 94°40′E

Dunhuang, Gansu.

Near Yanguan, Gansu.
A cemetery.

39°56'N 94°02'E

Beacon tower, salt flats.
Supplies depot, Dafangpan.
Beacon tower, Yanguan.

Between **39°56′N 94°02′E** and **40°20′N 93°42′E**

About 3000 feet above sea level.
Yumenguan, Dunhuang County, Gansu.
'The Jade Gate'.

40°21'N 93°52'E

Yumenguan, Dunhuang County, Gansu.
The Great Wall of the Han Dynasty.
Parallel with the Wall ran flat ditches filled with sand, the 'Heavenly Fields',
where any intruder would leave tracks.

40°21'N 93°46'E

Yumenguan, Dunhuang County, Gansu.
Westward to Lop Nor, the Great Wall was built with layers of bundled reed
alternating with clay mixed with pebbles.

40°21'N 93°46'E

Beyond Yumenguan, Gansu-Xinjiang border.
An end.

THE GREAT WALL IN HISTORY
AND HISTORICAL MAPS

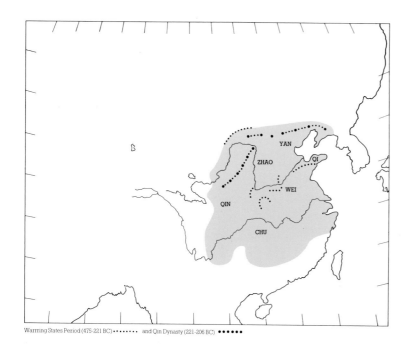

Warring States Period (475-221 BC) ········   and Qin Dynasty (221-206 BC) ●●●●●

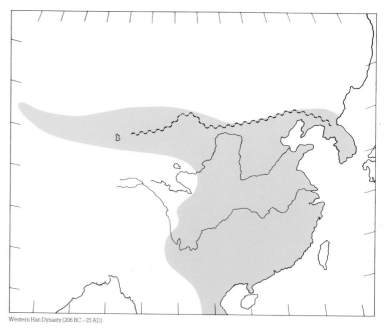

Western Han Dynasty (206 BC – 25 AD)

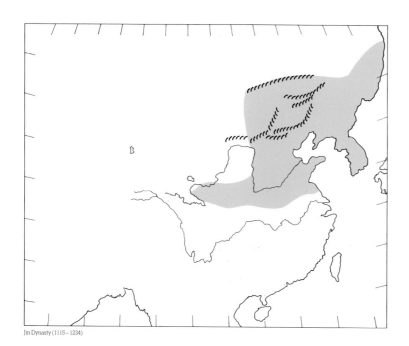

Jin Dynasty (1115 – 1234)

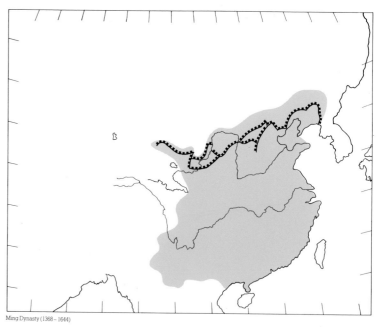

Ming Dynasty (1368 – 1644)

For centuries the Great Wall of China has been one of the wonders of the ancient world.

'There is no good man who has not been to the Great Wall' is a Chinese saying that has come to be used in praise of this great work of architecture not only by all the Chinese people, but also by foreign friends, experts and travellers.

The name of the Great Wall in Chinese is 'The Ten Thousand *li* Wall' (a *li* is a Chinese mile, about one third of an English mile) but it is actually far more than ten thousand *li* long. If we take the length of the Wall as first constructed and add on all the parts built by later dynasties, it is over 100,000 *li*. The scale of construction is without parallel, not only in China but anywhere in the world.

The Great Wall was not simply a defensive wall, nor was it merely a territorial boundary; it was an engineering feat combining defence, communications and other aspects, beacon towers and fortresses. Its many fortified gates, over 1000 castles and more than 10,000 beacons scattered within and without the Wall proper seem to fill the northern half of China. It was extended and restored according to the political and military requirements of each dynasty, whether their capitals were situated north, south, east or west. Today the Great Wall is ever-changing; passing over high mountain peaks, snaking across empty grassland plains or crossing the Gobi desert, rising and falling, twisting and dancing.

A long history

The construction of the Great Wall began in the 3rd century BC. It is by no means the oldest building of the ancient world but it has been constantly under construction for 2000 years, something that cannot be said of any other building in the world.

The history of the Great Wall is generally divided into two stages. The first stage is prior to the reign of the First Emperor of the Qin (who took power in 217 BC) and this is the Wall of the Spring and Autumn Period (770–476 BC) and the Warring States (476–221 BC), a period of China's history when many local rulers were fighting each other for power. The State of Chu was the first to build a wall in the 7th century BC, then the states of Qi, Zhongshan, Wei, Zheng, Han, Qin, Yan and Zhao all built walls of varying lengths. Some were less than 1000 *li*, some several 1000 *li* long.

The second period of the Wall's history dates from 217 BC when the Qin emperor unified the country, and in this phase, over 10 dynasties including the Qin, Han, Northern and Eastern Wei, Northern Qi, Northern Zhou, Sui, Liao, Jin, Yuan and Ming carried out building work on the Wall. The greatest periods of construction were during the Qin, Han, Jin and Ming. Work on the Wall under the first Qin emperor extended it to over 10,000 *li* so it only acquired its name of the 'Ten Thousand *li* Wall' from that period. The Han wall extended from the west bank of the Yellow River to the interior of Xinjiang province, and an outer wall was further constructed in the northern part; the full extent of both walls being over 20,000 *li* or 10,000 km. Under the Jin, the Wall was extended from Heilongjiang province to the banks of the Yellow River, an extension of some 10,000 *li*. The Ming was the last dynasty to undertake large-scale work on the Wall (some 7300 km.) and techniques were greatly improved. Many important sections were faced with brick to strengthen them. Most of what we see today is the Ming Wall. Throughout its 2000 year history, apart from the dynasties mentioned above, the Tang, Song and Qing also built and repaired the Wall according to their own needs, so we can say that the Great Wall has been constantly repaired and extended throughout its history.

Two points need to be stressed here. One is that in rebuilding the Wall, the aim of the first Qin emperor was to protect his empire from the Xiongnu [a non-Chinese group sometimes identified as Huns]. At the same time, he also ordered the destruction of the walls built by other states, to prevent them from re-arming themselves. The second point is that since China is a state of many nationalities, many rulers of minority nationality groups eventually achieved the exalted position of Emperor of China. After the Qin (217–210 BC) there were only three dynasties ruled by emperors of Chinese nationality that carried out substantial work on the Wall; the Han, Sui and Ming. Many more of the minority nationality-led dynasties (namely Northern and Eastern Wei, Northern Qi, Northern Zhou, Liao and Jin) worked on the Wall. Thus the Great Wall is the joint achievement of all of China's minority nationalities.

The importance of the Wall in China's history
Beginning with the Shang and Zhou dynasties 3–4000 years ago, the Yellow River plain and North China saw a succession of dynasties: Qin, Han, Sui, Tang, Song, Liao, Jin, Yuan, Ming and Qing. Their capitals and palaces, the heart of their government, were set up in the central Yellow River area, Shaanxi and Shanxi provinces and in Beijing. All the leaders of the minority nationalities that established dynasties came to the central plain in their struggle to gain the imperial position, whether they originated in the mountains of Shaanxi, the high plateau of Mongolia, the pine-covered Liaoning plain or south China. They came to the central Yellow River plain because the land there was fertile, science, technology and culture were highly developed, and all the conditions necessary to support the spiritual and material needs of government were met. No matter from which dynasty or which national minority a new leader came, his first main concern after establishing power was to maintain national security and assure the peaceful livelihood of his subjects. The greatest threats came from the horsemen from the north, north-east and north-west. They came like lightning and left like shooting stars and no generals could prevent them. From the Spring and Autumn and Warring States period (770–217 BC) and through the Qin and Han, the lesson that emerged from all these hundreds of years of experience was that the best form of defence against the sudden attacks of these fast-moving horsemen was to build defensive walls. Thus the construction of the Great Wall began and continued for thousands of years. Whether the ruling group were horsemen from the grasslands of Mongolia or mounted troops from the northern plains like the Northern Wei, Liao and Jin, once they had seized power and established their rule, they in their turn all repaired the Wall to protect their domains.

The Great Wall was generally successful in protecting the state and its inhabitants. During the Spring and Autumn period, when Qi attacked Chu, as soon as the troops saw the solid and imposing fortified wall, they retreated without joining battle. In the late Ming, when the latter Jin attacked Ningyuan on the eastern part of the Wall, the Ming general Yuan Chongyan would have been able to hold the town successfully by relying on the Wall had the troops at Shanhaiguan not surrendered to the Qing army: to take Shanhaiguan by simple military force would have been extremely difficult. Throughout its history, there are many such examples of the Great Wall's usefulness in withstanding enemy attacks and protecting the lands and peoples within it.

In its long history of many thousands of years, apart from its straightforward military usefulness, the Great Wall was also a factor in China's foreign relations, in the economic development of the north, in the unification of minority peoples, in cultural exchange and in many other ways. The 2nd century BC saw the establishment of the international trade route known as the 'Silk Road' which relied upon the protection of the Great Wall and its beacon fires to ensure unimpeded movement on the trade route. The arrival of settlers and the produce of the garrison's fields had a great impact on the sparsely populated and

Simatai, Miyun County, Beijing.
Restoration work in progress.

economically backward north of China, and most present-day cities along the Great Wall owe their existence to its protection. Because of the needs of the tens of thousands of garrison troops and Chinese settlers, the culture and products of the central plain and other areas were brought to the borders; at the same time, through the changing of garrisons and the movement of settlers and traders, the culture and products of the north were brought to the central plain and the rest of China, promoting cultural and economic exchange and development. In this and other historical aspects, the contribution of the Great Wall was immensely fruitful.

Military organization and communications

The military organization of the Wall was closely linked to its defensive role. Through the experience of thousands of years, it had become a unifying force that went from the centre outwards to the borders. The basic principle underlying the Wall was 'protect the land by dividing; control bit by bit, in sequence'. Taking the Ming wall as an example, the Wall of over 14,000 *li* was divided into twelve garrisons or military areas, each with a General Staff Headquarters as the highest level of authority, directed from the Board [or Ministry] of War. The size of each garrison depended upon the size of the area it had to control, from 10,000 to over 100,000 men (with a total of over a million soldiers). According to local needs, *lu* or circuits were set up below the General Staff Head-quarters, led by subordinate officers. A circuit would control some ten gate towers and a stretch of the Wall. Near the Wall, garrison towns were established as bases for the military personnel guarding the Wall. Within and without the Wall there were also numerous scattered fortifications, staffed by as few as ten or as many as a hundred soldiers, according to local terrain and defence requirements. The most basic form of garrison were those manning the watchtowers on the Wall itself and the beacons scattered on either side, which were staffed by duty groups who took turns to keep watch and make

patrols. Within this organization there were seven levels of administration. Military matters were communicated from the lowest level through the six superior levels to the Board of War through the Minister, and thence to the Emperor himself. The Emperor's orders were transmitted downwards through each level; this was part of the system of 'controlling bit by bit'.

Naturally, the coordination of the garrisons of this 10,000 *li* long Wall with its subordinate walls and territory was not without its problems. Military communication needed to be fast and accurate. Thus the beacon signalling system was perfected by military strategists of over 2000 years ago, using fire and smoke signals. The beacons have been given various names throughout Chinese history: beacon pavilions, smoke mounds or 'wolf smoke towers'. They were basically similar in construction, a platform ten metres high, made of tamped earth, stone or brick. Around the base there were dwellings, stores for the brushwood and animal pens. If enemies were spotted, smoke signals were used by day, fires by night. The number of enemy troops determined the size of the fires to be lit. This method of communication was instant; a message could be transmitted over 1000 *li* in minutes, from beacon to beacon to the General Headquarters, the Board of War and the Emperor himself. There were over 10,000 beacons in all, linking the Wall into a single unit.

Structure of the Wall

A great deal of experience in planning, engineering and use of materials was gathered over the thousands of years during which the Wall was constructed, extended and repaired. There are some singular aspects to its construction and engineering. The most important may be summarized in the phrase, 'Build according to the nature of the land; control narrow passes with strategic fortresses'. This is a saying that has been handed down throughout the 2000 years of the Wall's construction. In areas of high mountains and dangerous peaks, the height of the wall is altered according to the lie of the land and the local strategic requirements, making use of precipices or natural cliffs, with gullies and rivers serving as natural protective screens. Strategic gatehouses were situated in the places of greatest threat so that 'one man can hold the gate and ten thousand men cannot get through'.

As the area through which the Wall passes is vast, the geological environment is extremely varied: hence the maxim: 'Build according to the nature of the land and take materials from the land'. In high mountainous areas, stones were dug from the ground as the Wall was built and were used in its construction; in loess areas, tamped earth was used. The parts of the Wall that are brick-built used locally produced bricks. In the Gobi desert, the Wall was built from layers of red palm fronds, reeds and gravel. These methods all economized on transport and human labour. Today, traces of all these building methods still remain; some sections are stone-built, others made of tamped earth, brick and stone or palm frond and gravel.

The labourers who worked on the Wall were equally varied: there were the garrison troops, corvée labourers, military criminals and disgraced officials as well as craftsmen in brick, wood, earthworks and stone masonry. From early on, construction and maintenance were undertaken by local contract and the names of the soldiers who worked on particular sections at particular times can still be seen engraved on stone stelae on the watchtowers.

The Wall today
The historical usefulness of the Great Wall has completely disappeared today; the battlefields and defensive walls of the past can only serve as an occasional historical lesson.

But its magnificence and the solidity of its construction remain as an undying legacy for later generations. Apart from its usefulness as a tourist attraction and an object of historical research, the fabric of the Great Wall, indelibly marked by great natural events of the past – fissures caused by ancient earthquakes, traces of the movements of grasslands, desert and agriculture and the destruction of forests – serves as an accurate and eternal gauge of history and geography. To the scientist it is material for the study of the rules governing earthquakes, the stages of desertification and the growth of forests, and the knowledge gained from it helps to control the environment and maintain the ecological balance.

The Great Wall is a precious national and international archaeological relic and has been the object of considerable veneration. It is now protected in its entirety and important sections have been selected for renovation to be opened to both Chinese and foreign visitors. Apart from the investment of the Chinese government in the restoration of the Wall, financial help has been forthcoming from all sections of society both at home and abroad. A scientific study of the entire Wall is currently under way and we have already made many films and photographs and published many books on the Wall. But we still have not done enough to publicize this marvel.

We are confident that the publication of Mr. Schwartz's artistic photographs of the Wall will contribute to knowledge about it and make its outstanding visual qualities better known. This volume will increase understanding of China's ancient culture wherever it is published, and will greatly contribute to world friendship.

LUO ZHEWEN

The author would like to express his gratitude

To the local people, drivers and guides who directed me along the Walls.
To Luo Zhewen, Lecturer and Formerly Expert on Architecture at the State Bureau
of Cultural Relics and Museums in Beijing. His passion for the Great Wall also
became mine.
To Wang Dinkao of the Society for Research on the Great Wall in Beijing.
To Wang Jincheng in Shenyang, to Wang Yuecheng in Qinhuangdao, to Peng Siqi in
Beijing, to Xie Tingqui and Yuan Hairui in Datong, to Li Yiyou and Wang Xiaohua in
Hohhot, to Xu Cheng in Yinchuan, to Wu Renxian and Yue Bangfu in Lanzhou and to
Gao Fengshan in Jiayuguan. As Representatives of the Cultural Administration they
provided essential help.
To the Solothurnisches Kuratorium für Kulturförderung for granting a Werkjahr.
To Ilford Photo AG, Fribourg, to Nikon AG, Küsnacht, to Polaroid AG, Zurich, to
Yashica AG, Thalwil for their support.
And especially to my publisher for his encouragement and to all who worked on
this book.

Exhibition organized by the Musée de L'Elysée, Lausanne:

Dortmund, Museum am Ostwall   August 12 – November 11, 1990
Lausanne, Musée de l'Elysée   February 5 – March 31, 1991